I SURVIVED!

TRUE ENCOUNTER OF A BATTERED WOMAN

By

Adrianne D. Brady

NEW REVISED EDITION 2018

Copyright© 2006 by Adrianne D. Brady

ISBN: **0964644266**

May 2006

Library of Congress Control Number: 2005908757

All rights reserved. No part of this book may be used or reproduced by any means without prior written permission of the owner.

Published by Adrianne D. Brady

Original Edits by: Rhongelyn Moore Narh and Malcolm Barr

Revision Edits by: Pastor Evelyn King, Reverend Janice Cummings Rhongelyn Moore Narh & Gisel Samuels, James Johnson

Revised Edition 2015 Edits by Ronda Buckmon

Revised Edition Cover Design and Book Format by Wanda Alston creativebyhisdesign@gmail.com

All Scripture References:	The Thompson Chain-Reference Bible Fifth Improved Edition
Commentary:	Matthew Henry Commentary unless otherwise noted.

Printed in the United States of America
I Brady Solutions

Contact Author: 202-644-6741 email:adriannebrady@yahoo.com

New Revised Edition 2006
New Revised Edition 2013
New Revised Edition 2018

7th Print

Table of Contents

Dedication x
Introduction xii
Chapter 1 - Life Before the Abuse 1
   The Meeting 2
Chapter 2 - A Strong Delusion 6
   Drastic Change 7
   My Job Didn't Take It So Well 10
Chapter 3 - Enduring Until the End 13
   God Bless the Children 16
   Eviction 17
Chapter 4 - The Light at the End of the Tunnel 22
Chapter 5 – Free! Free! Free! At Last 24
   New Beginnings 25
Chapter 6 – A Fresh Start 28
   One Day At A Time 29
Chapter 7 – Transition 31
Chapter 8 – Church 35
Chapter 9 – A New Partner 37
   More Healing To Be Done 39
Chapter 10 – Road To Recovery 41
   Moving On 44
Chapter 11 – Time for Ministry 47
Epilogue 51
   Survival Strategies 51
   Are You Being Abused? 53
   Scriptural References 55

DEDICATION

This Revised Edition of I Survived, True Encounter of a Battered Woman is dedicated to the Body of Christ. Through all that God has allowed me to endure, I count it a privilege to share my story. We must take back our families, and do it with the love of God. If we are who we say we are, then, let the redeemed of the Lord say so.

Introduction

As I began to write my story, I had many flashbacks; some good, most painful. I realize the only way I am able to share these experiences is because of my spiritual growth and the grace of God. I thank God for the strength that He has given me to write. I pray that others will be uplifted.

This story is not written to slander or hurt anyone in any way. I only pray that what I've experienced will help others and bring deliverance to both the men and the women who will read it.

God is not the author of confusion! While writing this story, I was faced with many uncertainties about many things. My main question was, "Why Lord, why me?" In this Christian walk, we experience many things, not all of them pleasing. We can't argue with God, even though our physical bodies may be affected. Since I have been delivered, I see things more clearly.

There is a great deception going on in the body of Christ. This book will reveal some of the things I've encountered. I pray that it will offer hope and encouragement to those who are, and those striving to be, part of the body of Christ.

The person that I was married to was an ordained minister. He knew God's word. He had lived God's word. Most of the abuse I suffered at his hands was based on references he gave me from scripture. The Bible was literally thrown at me. Every other line he used was scripture. I wanted to know God so badly that I was easily influenced. I accepted my husband's word, not because I didn't know whether it was from God, but because I knew that the scriptures he used could be interpreted by others (clergy), the same way he used them. Through study of God's word, I am enlightened with knowledge to teach and help others. God is not pleased with what we are allowing in the body of Christ. There is urgency for the body of Christ to seek God's word for guidance concerning domestic violence in the church.

There were many times during the abuse when I turned to the church for help. The church I attended didn't know what to do! The church sent me back to my husband. This doesn't mean that the church was wrong, but because of the situation, it didn't know what to do. The church acted out of ignorance. The attitudes and actions of those around me led me to believe that there is very little knowledge as to how to counsel an abused or abusive person. Many believe that it is the woman's fault for staying in the relationship and that she can easily escape if she wants to. This too is indicative of the lack of information distributed throughout society concerning victims of abuse.

Television depicts a perpetrator with the same characteristics as the real life abuser. The perpetrator's behavior is duplicated. Yet there is a sense of, "oh no, if that were me I'd leave," or "why doesn't she leave?" Instead of asking the question, "Why does he do it?"

The Bible says, "God made man first, woman last" and in their sinful state, her desire would be towards her husband, and he shall rule over her (Gen 3:16). This was her punishment for disobedience. This scenario could leave women powerless. This "to rule over" line can be interpreted by some to never question his actions and to be watched over in order to live righteously. This would imply that we (women) were an afterthought and are yet being punished for the initial sin. God did make man first. He made woman from man to be his helpmate. God used Adam's rib. As stated in the commentary of 17th century minister and author, Matthew Henry, "(God) did not make her from his head to be above him. He did not make her from his feet to be trampled upon. Instead, he made her from his side to be an equal." Although women may not be able to accomplish the tasks that God put in the hands of men, it doesn't mean that we can't significantly contribute. Also, this is not an indication that we should never question man's ability to lead.

Women have come a long way. During the Levitical era women were barred from the church. There was a place for them called "Court of the Women" or Treasury (where the offering was taken). This was an open court. However, when Jesus made his triumphal entry (Matthew 21:1-15) to Jerusalem, he went through the Court of Women. After Jesus had ministered to many of the women, (the widow's mite, the sinful woman) they became witnesses and followers. They then felt led to tell (preach) others of the goodness of Jesus, they oversaw (pastor) ministries on behalf of the apostle, and shared (taught) their experiences with those who would hear, even the men (St. John 4:29).

Once women were allowed in the church, they gained strength through the word of God and became prayer warriors. Over the years, women have proven their faithfulness and diligence in the ways of God by the trying of his word. This is evident in the number of women in the local church today, and the gifts that are being exercised through them. This in some ways intimidates men. If God can use a donkey, he can use a woman (Matthew 21:2-3). Where is her place?

Abuse exists every day and in many different ways. There's physical, mental, verbal, sexual, and last but not least, spiritual abuse. Yes, spiritual abuse exists. When a woman is led to believe that God speaks only to a man, or she has no place in Christ, this is spiritual abuse. Many women are in bondage today because of their misleading interpretation of some of the most common scriptures given to exclude them. 1Peter 3:1 says "wives be in subjection to your own husbands...," and 1Timothy 2:11 & 12 says "let the woman learn in silence....". The meaning of these scriptures has been taken out of context and misinterpreted by many.

Yes, we are to be in subjection to our husbands according to scripture, but the entire scripture must be considered in order to see the blessing. By being in subjection (acknowledging the authority given to him by God) she finds herself being a blessing to him whether he is within or without Christ in his life. He then may be won (to the Lord) by the conversations of the wives.

1Timothy 2:11 says, "Let the woman learn in silence with all subjection." During that period, women were new to the church. While they were now allowed to attend, many of these women did not know how to conduct themselves in the congregation. Some asked questions out of order. So that things could be done, as God would have them, in decency and order, Paul gave the aforementioned instruction to Timothy for the Church.

Jesus has given many illustrations where he used a woman, not to make a man feel uncomfortable, but to help him. There are more women in the church today. If man won't do his job, then the scripture says, "**whosoever**" will come after me, let him deny himself, and take up his cross, and follow me" (Mark 8:34), which would imply either gender.

Also, Galatians 3:26-29 says, we **all** are children of God by faith in Jesus Christ ... there is neither male nor female: for we are all one in him.

Chapter 1 - Life Before the Abuse

Growing up was hard for me. I had very low self-esteem. There were many uncertainties in my young life. I remember always trying to do things that would please someone else in an effort to be accepted. Above all, I wanted to love and be loved. I remember in third grade, I was telling the other children that I loved them. Of course, they laughed, then someone asked, "how do you love me when you don't know me?" My response was, "God wants us to love everyone and so do I."

I grew up in two different environments. The one I got my discipline and religious direction from was my grandparents' house. We went to church every Sunday, which whetted my interest in serving the Lord. I remember visiting my grandparents most weekends and holidays. I enjoyed being there. I got to play outside, ride my bike, and go to amusement parks for picnics. Although there were incidents that I wish I could forget. I was the youngest girl who stayed in the house, so when we played house I was always the mother and the mother had to please the father. I guess one would say children will be children and experiment with what they think they know. Well, this was much deeper than child play. I never told anyone for fear of what would happen. I had witnessed so much violence already, at both my parents' and grandparents house, that I was very nervous. I thought that if I told, then I would be found at fault and an argument or fight would break out.

In the other environment, my parents' house, I had a little more freedom. I could basically come and go as I pleased. I did have to let my parents know where I was, but most of the time, without them knowing, I did as wished. I enjoyed myself a lot more at my parents' house. I had my own bedroom with a television and record player, which was unique during that time, because most of my friends had to share everything. At my grandparent's house we had to share everything and ate one-pot meals (because there were many mouths to feed).

I knew that my parents and grandparents loved me, but I had emptiness that I needed to be fulfilled – to be wanted, needed, hugged and loved. This void made me vulnerable to a lot of misuse and abuse later in my life. I really believe that if I could have heard those three words, "I love you," enough when I was growing up that it would have had a major effect on the some of the decisions that I made in my adult life.

I was determined to be the center of attention. I began doing things that I thought would make me attractive. Since growing up all that seemed to interest men was my body. So if that meant I could use my body to get what I wanted, then I did. The married man, with the strongest will not to commit adultery, became a challenge. I tempted until he gave in.

As I reflect on my life, I realize now that God not only blessed me but he saved me from myself. I thought, "I must do this and I must do it right." The Lord has brought me a mighty long way, and I owe Him. Little did I know this race was just getting started!

The Meeting

The Lord had given me another chance to surrender my life completely to Him. I accepted the Lord as my personal Savior in June 1982. I had been up and down with the Lord for more than four years, saved one day, unsaved the next day. I wasn't sure how I wanted to live, for God or Satan. One day in October 1985, the Lord opened my eyes to myself. I realized that although I was in the church I was no better than those who had never thought about serving God. My life was unstable and incomplete. I needed Jesus. The things that I was doing were not pleasing in His sight.

I found a church where I really felt the presence of the Lord. I was growing in the Lord and things were beginning to change positively for me. I had a boyfriend who attended church with me, but I separated myself from him. I let him know that we could no longer disobey God's word. During a nightly devotion service, I openly made it clear that I was going to serve God until I die. I did not know it at the time but my future husband was in the congregation when this announcement was made.

I was 24, a single parent of two daughters, ages 2 and 4. I worked full-time and was enrolled in college part-time. I was also two months into my first apartment and pretty proud of myself. I really believed that God was blessing me and that I was now, finally, on the right road.

I finally saw my prospective husband in my church. After hearing so much about him, I thought, "sure looks good." This man was very attractive and very polite. I noticed that he appeared to be very spiritual and confident in his belief in God. He worked for the church, which won the hearts of the Pastor, First Lady, and our small congregation.

Later, I discovered that he had once been a Pastor in the South and was yet working in the Ministerial capacity. He had moved to the area less than a year before and was trying to get settled. He initially lived with relatives but was staying at a homeless shelter when I met him.

As I think back, I didn't much like him at first. Yes, he was handsome but that wasn't what attracted me to him. At that time, I was really getting my life to where I wanted it to be in the eyes of the Lord. He seemed to have a spiritual zeal that I so desperately wanted which would enable me to win souls and to do God's Will. I thought, "well, if God wants me to have him, then he would give him to me."

He taught Sunday school and joined the choir. He preached and strived to win souls for Christ in these and other ways. More and more I became interested in him. It seemed he had no problem believing in God for whatever he desired. He loved the Lord. That's what I wanted and I thought he was who I needed. He got along with everybody. People enjoyed his company. He was a perfect gentleman. I could see why he attracted so much attention. He appeared to captivate his audience wherever he went.

I found out later that he stayed in the homeless shelter by choice because he was active in being an advocate for the shelter. He was a member of the volunteer board at the shelter, which was led by some distinguished city officials. Through this position, he became well known, and familiar with very important local government people.

He was 12 years older than me, had been married before and had told me that our marriage would be a new beginning for him. We would be the family of God.

Our relationship started like most relationships in the church; we fellowshipped together. It was obvious that other women in the church were also interested in him. Some came to church specifically because he was there. Some admitted to me that they were attracted to him. I somehow knew that I would be the one who ended up with him.

We had spent most of our nights getting to know each other before we got married. He would visit late at night and would want to talk. We would talk into the early morning hours. As a result, most of the time, I was late going to work. He would cook breakfast for me and iron my clothes for work. When I got home from work, dinner would be ready. He was winning me over. I had never had anyone be this nice to me. Everything was great.

CHAPTER 2 - A STRONG DELUSION

IN THE BEGINNING, his spiritual confidence captivated me. If he fasted for a week, I fasted for a week. If he said God told him something, I believed him. When he read a scripture, he made it seem so easy to apply. I wanted the same spirit. I wanted what he had with God, and I just knew that only the Lord could send this person in my life to help me get closer to Him. It was as if God was opening up this door exclusively for me. He seemed to have all the qualities of a true child of God that I desired. Even when he spoke to me, he knew exactly what to say and how to say it.

One encounter I recall was this: I was fairly new to my apartment, and I started having problems with tithes and paying rent. I felt within myself that I should tithe first, no matter what. I asked him what he thought, and he said exactly what I wanted to hear. Everything that I had wondered about concerning the ways of God he seemed to know the answer. I knew that only God could have given this man to me. Only God knew what was in my heart. My desire to completely serve Him was being fulfilled. I totally subjected myself to this man (for knowledge) before we married. I knew that this was God's way of giving me His wisdom.

He enticed me by saying things that captivated me; not only about myself but his experiences with God. I had been involved in a physical relationship prior to meeting him, but decided I wanted the things of God. He helped me to understand that God understood a lot of my emotions and that I was forgiven and set free. This enabled me to justify my relationship with him when it became physical before we were married.

The way that he carried himself was exceptionally different from what I had been used to. He seemed to have a sense of purity in his relationship with God.

I knew the Lord was going to make this thing "right," and move us up higher in Him together. Well, "right" it got, because two months later we were married and I was one month pregnant. I really thought this was God's purpose for my life.

Drastic Change

He asked me what I would say if he asked me to marry him. I told him I would say, "yes." He then replied, well, let's get married. That line was followed by "we won't tell anyone until we are married." I accepted and made plans to be married. We were married at another church because of the suspicions in the congregation of our seeing each other. Although he did make an announcement in church before we were married that I was his fiancé, I didn't consider why everything was so hush, hush. I was just going with what he said. The people at my job were surprised. I didn't even tell my mother until I came back from the church on my wedding day. Now that I think about it, I guess I was captivated by this man's attention and the sincerity that I felt from him in loving me. I really thought that he was all about me, and I enjoyed it. I thought that this was the happiest day of my life. God had not only given me a husband, but a man of God, and not a bench member. God had blessed me. After the initial surprise, some congratulated me. But then, things began to change and change rapidly.

He began questioning me on just about everything. He wanted to know about my friends, my family, my likes and dislikes. He especially wanted to know about my life in sin. At first, this did not bother me, but quickly things began unraveling, coming apart.

About four months into the relationship, things got even worse. I was now showing signs of both my pregnancy and the mental abuse. Instead of gaining weight, which is normal during pregnancy, I started losing weight. I was getting smaller and smaller! My friends hardly recognized me. I was the talk of the workplace. No one knew for sure what was going on.

I did not know I was being brainwashed. I was being made to believe that I was his wife unconditionally. He told me it was none of my friends business what he or I did.

He constantly bombarded me with questions. I gave him the best answers I could. I gave him the truth. However, he soon began to correct my answers by interpreting the answers I gave. My life continued to deteriorate.

If the telephone rang and it was a wrong number, immediately he concluded that it was a boyfriend. He wanted to know when I had last spoken to or seen any of my former boyfriends. I answered him truthfully. I told him when I had seen one of my former boyfriends and that nothing happened, that provoked further arguments, and he acquired instant symptoms of having a venereal disease. I was blamed for that. I thought, "What is going on?" He asked me constantly, if I had slept with this man. I told him no and tried to explain that my life was different now. I knew that I wasn't living all that God had required. However, I also knew that my days of fornication and adultery had ended when I decided to live seriously for the Lord.

But that was not enough. The all night questioning sessions continued. Finally, it dawned on me that the only way out of this hell was to admit to his suspicions. Although it wasn't true, I gave in. I confessed to having committed adultery for the sake of peace. He acknowledged that he had known this because he couldn't have gotten the venereal disease any other way. According to him, he was not sleeping with anyone before me. At last I was allowed to get some rest. I had lied just to get a little sleep. The lies kept coming. The first lie, told out of fear, was the beginning of Hell on earth. Miraculously, his venereal disease symptoms disappeared. I concluded he must have cured himself because he never went to see a doctor and neither did I.

From that time on it was fight after fight, lie after lie. I was hit, slapped, kicked. These fights were very physical. It didn't start with a slap. It started with me being picked up and thrown down on my head for inviting my sister and her boyfriend over. He concluded that because I invited my sister and her boyfriend over, that meant I had invited the first man to our house since we got married. I was beat, my sister and her friend never did come over.

Suddenly the church where he had found so much favor and demonstrated so much spiritual zeal was no longer good enough for us. We could no longer fellowship in that church. As the man of the house, he stated he had to select the church for his family. Slowly, we began to withdraw further into his world. My outside world was vanishing fast.

We became caught up in his world. All this time, he didn't work. He had a medical case pending with the Veteran's Administration that meant he couldn't work until he got a disability decision. So, he seemed to spend all day when he should have been working, thinking of ways to harass me.

I started noticing certain changes in his behavior. He had become overwhelmingly talkative. He was naturally a talker, but now he made me at last aware of what he was doing to make him so energetic. One day I was at work and I got a call from my husband. He was acting very strange. He and my baby girl, who was 2, (he babysat since he had no job) were talking loud on the telephone. It was as if the call was someone playing on the telephone. They laughed and laughed. I knew that this could be natural behavior for my daughter; she was only a child. But he just seemed too much out of place. I was so afraid I left work and went home. I, not surprisingly, found he was just high as he could be. This is when I realized he was using some form of drug. I found out later that the drug was called "love boat", some form of marijuana laced with embalming fluid. Now it really got scary and more confusing than ever. He justified his drug use with "God is not that narrow-minded that he would hold you accountable for something that doesn't have a mind of its own." The key is, he said, "you control the drug and not let the drug control you." Of course I was the reason he smoked it! However, I did notice that whenever he used drugs he would leave me alone. Most of the time, he would smoke and then go outside and preach.

As time went by, the drug abuse became more frequent. He even started drinking. Indirectly, the drugs helped me a lot; because when he was high, he went out, or even if he stayed home he would not fight me, but he sure would talk me to death. I found myself working, coming home and giving him my paycheck so that he would get drugs, get high and leave me alone.

My Job Didn't Take It So Well

I began missing time from work. I was accused of being unfaithful at work. This made it even more difficult for me to function. I had the only paycheck coming in, and it was short every two weeks because of the time I was missing. During that first year of marriage, I don't believe I ever received a full check.

My supervisor and I did not get along prior to my marriage but, now, he seemed even more demanding. My working relationships seemed to always end in arguments. At the time, I was also attending college in the evening. This also became a source of problems. My husband insisted I drop out since I "wasn't learning anything anyway," he would say.

Then my home problems began to have even more of an effect on my job. If I had to call in sick, he listened to the conversation. We only had one telephone and if the tone of voice from the other person from my job sounded too nice then that person had to have been intimate with me (male or female). At my husband's insistence, I filed grievance papers against my supervisor. Although, I was having problems with my supervisor, I hadn't planned to file a grievance, however, in an effort to show him that I was committed to making the marriage work, the grievance papers were filed.

My husband became my advocate. He attended all meetings on my behalf. He wrote letters excusing my absences. The friends I ate lunch with became people who merely existed. I wasn't supposed to have any further dealings with them. Some of them began to perceive my actions as very strange. One of them went so far as to call adult protection and child protection services on my behalf. This action later forced me to undergo mental evaluation in my home because of my questionable behavior. I was accused of telling people I was carrying a dead fetus inside of me, which was not true. I later realized that they were trying to make the government intervene on my behalf. However, this opened up a court case against me. Although I passed their examinations and evaluations I was yet tormented with the fact that the government began trying to take my children away from me based on child abuse allegations. Ironically, I was the one being abused.

I continued to pray but things didn't get better. My husband forbade me to communicate with people. I couldn't speak to anyone. If people passed by while I was talking to my husband on the telephone, he demanded to know whom I was talking to and what they said.

An incident on the job resulted in my husband being banned from the building. He approached one of the men who I worked with about talking down to me about him. Whereas, I was trying to show my husband how I defended him to those who spoke against him. Well, when he approached this man, the man offered to take him outside to settle it. Things got loud, and my husband declared that he was non-violent and that he let God fight his battles. My husband was now banned from the building, which only added one more man's name to the list of those who I had sexual relations with on my job. The work place caused even more problems at home — It meant he could not sneak up on me and catch me in the so-called "act."

My husband's actions indicated that something was definitely wrong, more than just drugs. Jealousy was a major issue. He seemed intimidated by anyone who was close to me. He found something wrong with all of my friends and co-workers. He alienated them all. He managed to get me to believe that it was them and not him. When I appeared to stand up for myself at work, he convinced me that they were angry with me. He assured me that he was with me all the way. I later realized that his techniques in justifying himself were effective because of the information that I had given him during my period of complete honesty.

Through it all, I continued to pray. I asked God to help me to make the marriage work.

Chapter 3 - Enduring Until the End

In spite of all of the trauma, I excused all of my husband's actions because; I believe that he loved me. He was special and, since he was new to the area, he needed some extra attention. If my friends weren't good enough for him then that was fine. He was my husband whom God had given me and I must respect his wishes even to the exclusion of my mother, sister and brother.
"A man should leave his father and mother and cleave unto his wife" (Gen. 2:24). He would never let any of his or my relatives offend me. I believed it important that I learn that marriage meant oneness. And included in that was the proposition that we would have our ups and downs, maybe even physical fights, but through it all God would bring us through. This was my attitude. This was my belief. If God had chosen this man for me, and we were going to do great things for God together, then we had to suffer some things. He would work it out.

In addition to my changing relations with my friends, co-workers, and family, he also demanded that I change my attire. He believed that since I was his wife, I was his queen. No one, he concluded, should be allowed to see my body but him. I had a calling, he said, to exemplify the ways of a pure, virtuous woman of God. Patterning myself after Sarah "The Mother of Nations" who obeyed Abraham, calling him Lord; I was to dress accordingly. If this would please my husband, then it would be done. I started by covering my head. I was his glory. I went from covering my head to covering my body. He made my outfits from whatever he found available. I was his queen. Whatever it took to make him understand that I was not the person he said that I was, I was willing to do. I was determined that through God, someway, somehow, he would know that he was wrong in all that he believed about me.

The fights became more frequent. I was thrown over chairs. I was now being tied up and hit. My hands were tied behind me, and my feet were tied together. I was constantly questioned about everything. If my answer wasn't what he thought it should be, then I was lying. Again, I thought maybe if I agreed with him he would see that it didn't matter what I had done. I told him that all I wanted to do was to be right in the eyes of God and that I would not cover up just to save others. After I confessed that I had done whatever precipitated the fight, I was showered with gifts: fresh flowers, fresh bath water, back rubs, and facials. He would use his remedies for the scars because I wasn't allowed to go to the hospital. After each fight we had "honesty time." I was to confess, he would be sorry; he would try to believe me. He would never hit me again. We would pray. We always prayed, and played Gospel music. We stayed before the Lord. We even had in-home church service for the family. Whenever I was the speaker, I was not allowed to talk about anything that didn't pertain to the women of the Bible. That was not my place.

At this time, I began to see the seriousness of my deteriorating situation. My husband was now becoming jealous of God. I was told that I could pray to God but only through him. I couldn't go to God myself. I was out of order.

I don't know how, according to him, I stayed in so much trouble when most of my time (99 percent) was spent in his presence. I stayed home. When we did have money, he did the shopping.

Next, problems began to crop up in our neighborhood. I knew the neighbors only by seeing them; he said I knew them more than I had acknowledged. He started talking to some of them. According to him, they knew all about my past life, and were talking behind his back as to how much I'd fooled him. He accused me of seeing several men who lived in our apartment building.

One in particular, I was beaten badly for. One minute I said I did it and the next five minutes I declared I hadn't. Talk about brainwashing, confusion! Now my husband continued to talk to this very man he beat me up for allegedly having sex with. One night the man knocked on the door. I answered and he asked for my husband. My husband was home but I pretended that he wasn't. I wanted to get this man to talk and convince my husband that I didn't know him from Adam. I told the man that he needed to tell the truth, and to stop being around my husband. The man was so confused; he started telling me I was crazy, and that I needed to see a doctor.

After about a half an hour, my husband opened the door and let him in, and he explained what was going on. My husband told him that he now believed that I didn't have sex with this man. Totally confused! The neighbor wasn't the only one. I told another man's wife that I had been with her husband when I hadn't. I don't think she believed me, because she heard many of the fights we had and was aware of the abuse.

I continued to trust God to either bring me out or take me home. I remember being by myself praying. I would always find myself singing and praising God. Looking back, I don't know why I felt content since I wasn't sure when my husband came home whether he would be mad or glad. I never knew. All that I was sure of was that when he left I had peace. I know that the children did also. When he came home, they were made to stay in the bedroom a lot. Sometimes if he came home mad, they wouldn't eat for hours. He would sometimes fight me all night long. I neither rested nor slept. I was always tired. I was hit with everything in the house, the broom, the mop, a stick, or a pole. Most of the furniture we had was destroyed. I was stabbed, hot rice was thrown at me, I was urinated on, and I was bitten on my back and feet. I made many attempts to leave with and sometimes without the children. Where was I going? Everyone thought I was angry and didn't want help. Finally, when things became hopeless, I began to pray that the Lord would help me out of this marriage that I had chosen.

God Bless the Children

Initially, my daughters, who were 2 and 4, were apprehensive about him. The anxiety lasted a short time. But then it became very quiet at our house. Where I used to hear them laughing and playing, it got totally silent. The girls weren't allowed to be children. They had to be quiet. As a result, they became introverted. Before, they were always running and playing; now they were made to remain in their rooms. My oldest daughter suffered the most. She did well in school but where she was once very talkative, she became very quiet. He constantly drilled and questioned her about my activities. She was accused of knowing too much about sex and being sneaky. This was concluded when he would find her lying on the floor in the morning instead of being in her bed. Well, I tried to tell him that she was used to looking for me if I wasn't in the bed when she woke up. So in her search for me she would fall asleep on the floor near the couch where we slept. He thought that her motive for being there was that she was trying to see us having sex.

While she was allowed to continue in school, her 2-year-old sister was removed from day care so that he could watch her, since he wasn't working. The children changed to the point that I really couldn't tell what they were feeling. Although he wasn't physically abusive to the girls I knew that they were afraid.

All of this time I was pregnant! Although I did get to go to all of my doctor's appointments, they, too, were really concerned about me because I wasn't gaining weight. They gave me food vouchers. I was given dietary supplements, anything to help my appetite. They didn't know of the stress I was under.

When I went into labor I had just been beaten and I didn't know that I was in labor. I thought that my back was hurting because of him fighting me. I guess I had gotten used to pain. I gave birth to my son at home. He weighed 5 lbs. and that was all that I had gained over the 9 months. I had to go to the hospital with a black eye. My husband tormented me by telephone while I was in the hospital. There was no peace anywhere.

When I returned home, the abuse continued. This time it included the baby. My husband would toss the baby from the crib to our bed. I believed he wasn't trying to hurt the baby intentionally, but I knew that he could hurt him accidentally.

I was more determined now than ever to leave, if not for myself then for the sake of my children.

Eviction

Of course since I wasn't able to go to work, we couldn't keep the rent paid. That day finally came. Everything I had was gone. I thought this would be the end of the fights and maybe he would think seriously about our life since we had nowhere to live. Wrong, wrong, wrong again. It continued. It worsened.

At first we lived on the streets. We went to the shelters but they didn't have enough room. He insisted that we sleep together in the same room. He was not going to let his family sleep in a big room full of people. We were going to sleep on the mayor's steps! There we were at the District Building in our Nation's Capital. This was the most embarrassing time. I learned to be abased. I learned to have and to not have. I know first-hand the treatment of the homeless. I always believed that if things really got bad I could go home to my mother, but the protective service agency told me that my mother was the lead person in trying to have my children taken away from me.

There was an incident that occurred in downtown D.C., which gave the protective service cause to summons us to court in reference to our children. This happened one day while we were sitting on a step. My husband began preaching, and the children and I were sitting down listening. I took out a diaper to change my baby when suddenly a man came and gave me some money. At first I wouldn't take it, thinking, "what is this for"? Then my husband said, take it, we need it, so I did. Money then started pouring in. Well, lo and behold, one of my relatives came downtown and saw people giving us money, and decided that we were begging. What did he do? He called my mother and told her that we were asking people for money. Lies, all lies but we were required to go to the police precinct with our children and prove that we had shelter. Once we proved that we had a place to go, they took us to the shelter where we were staying.

Since my husband knew some city officials he called them for favors. Some of the people he knew who worked for the government gave us money when we needed it. We were able to get into second phase shelter for families who have been in the main shelter awhile, ahead of many people who had been on the waiting list for years. A short time afterward, we received our first summons to appear in court. The summons said we were downtown preaching on the street with our children who were dirty and that it was 98 degrees. The agency wanted to take the children.

We tried to find a way to fight the case, but we knew we were in danger of losing them because we didn't really have adequate shelter. My husband contacted his relatives and explained our situation. He made it appear that my mother was the problem.

Everything he seemed to say and do was all right with me, because I knew we were not wrong. His relatives told us to bring the children to them and go fight our case. They lived out-of-state. The judge had already told the protective service that they were treading on thin ice and that they needed more evidence than what they had to take the children from us. It was the beginning of a long haul. We were given another date to bring them to court. They were put in the custody of the relatives with whom they were staying. We soon had to leave the second phase shelter because we didn't have the children with us. Through all of this, the fights and the abuse continued. Instead of fighting the government, he was fighting me!

It wasn't long after the eviction that I officially lost my job. I received a lump sum of money from the government by applying for my severance pay. The children were no longer with us, they were with his family.

We were able to stay in a hotel for a few nights (10 days of no abuse!) and buy a car. After the hotel money ran out, our car was our house. And, of course, the fights began again. During the time spent outside, in shelters and in the car, I had more black eyes; my head was stomped on, I was beat with the lug wrench, punched, and kicked in my vagina. I was hospitalized for a miscarriage, when it was actually a blood clot from where he kicked me. I was tormented by his voice on the telephone while in the hospital. There was nowhere to run, nowhere to hide. Only God knew.

So many different things were going on along with the abuse. Through the grace of God, the enemy did not overtake me. I could see God through everything. My strength was found in Isaiah 54:17, "No weapon that is formed against thee shall prosper..."

My husband did what he could to patch me up before court dates. We had less and less contact with the children. We began gypsy cabbing. The more people we drove around, the more of them I was accused of knowing. The court cases were coming to an end and he was fighting me more and more, I constantly had black eyes.

We were back and forth to the court. The lawyer assigned to represent the children had to do an in-home visit out of town. We had attorneys that the court appointed for us. He was angry because they gave us two separate attorneys. He made them work together. We could not have separate meetings; he wouldn't hear of it. We waited for the report from the government attorney who would determine whether the children were in danger or not.

    I recall one time while preparing to go to court. He had been getting high all day. Well, he ran out of drugs and money and he asked me if I knew someone who we could get money from. I told him that I didn't. He knew that I had an aunt who came to see me at different times and because of the state of mind that I was in, I would never let her in the house or would talk to her because of embarrassment. But she never stopped stretching her hands out for me. Somehow I allowed him to coerce me into going to see my aunt and asking her for money but to say that I needed it to stay in a hotel for the night in order to prepare for court. This was the hardest thing that I had to do. First of all, I knew that this was a lie. He wanted drugs. Well, I went to my aunt's house and I felt so uncomfortable that I didn't wait for her to come downstairs. I just ran out the house crying. I didn't want my aunt to see me like this, and I didn't want to lie to her. She came running out of the house saying, don't go, what you need. I was so embarrassed and so hurt. I told her what I needed and she gave it to me and I left. This was devastating and I knew I had to leave him. It was extremely hard for me to face my aunt after that episode. He ended up trying to buy drugs and what he bought wasn't drugs at all. They sold him soap instead of crack cocaine. So he still didn't get what he wanted. He wasted the money.

    We were due back in court for the final time. We arrived early. The prosecutor greeted us with an agreement for us to sign. Apparently, they couldn't find anything wrong with our children. The agreement stated that if we brought the children back to this area, that we would make sure that they were in the best care. We would take them to the doctor regularly, and would have a stable shelter for them. The agreement sounded as though they were giving us options because the children were in their care, but this was not so. My husband told the prosecutor to delete the line that says we must comply according to the protective service, as though they had custody. The prosecutor did exactly what he asked. The bottom line? They didn't have enough evidence to take our children. Case closed. Thank you, Jesus!

The time had come for me to be delivered. It was February, and I wanted my children and my life back.

CHAPTER 4 - THE LIGHT AT THE END OF THE TUNNEL

WE HAD JUST DROPPED OFF A PASSENGER. I was accused of knowing the passenger and trying to communicate with him. During this time I had a black eye and it was so bad that I couldn't keep my dark glasses on. I did not want to be hit anymore. I refused to be beaten again. I had done nothing for two years but try to make this work. Through all the pain, I wanted to make it work. I really tried, but that day, I was fed up and said, "no more!" He was furious. He was so mad that he stopped the car. When he got out of the car, I slid over into the driver's seat and pulled off. I heard his voice trailing off. As I screamed, "I didn't do it, I didn't do it, and I didn't do it!"

I rode around for two days. Not knowing where to go and without anything to eat. I slept in the car. I wasn't going back to him. I even tried to panhandle but I couldn't. Nobody would help me. They looked at me funny. I was hungry and I didn't know where to turn. I slept in the parking lot. I finally decided to tell someone. I needed to talk to my children. I called his relatives and told them what was going on. I told them that I didn't have any money but I was going to find a job and would come to pick up my children. God was with me. They decided to wire me some money. The only Western Union in the area was near where we had been staying. I finally got up enough courage to go pick it up. After I picked up the money, and was leaving the office, who should I see, but him. "Oh no, Lord," I said to myself. "Please Lord, no more. Please Lord."

He had seen the car while riding on the bus. He insisted I go with him. I refused. No more, I told him. He wouldn't let me go. Finally, I told him the only way that I would ride with him would be if he would go with me right now to get my children. He agreed. Of course we had to stop to take care of a few things, tags, gas, and of course drugs with the money that I had gotten.

All seemed to be fine as long as he was high. Then it started. I was beaten for two of the three hundred miles we traveled. I was made to get out of the car, then he would drive away and come back to get me. I endured because I had made up my mind.

We finally arrived and I understood why God had sent him to go with me. There were incidents that occurred that I would not have been able to handle alone, such as the flat tire, checking the oil, and so on.

We stayed at his parent's house before the door was finally opened. When it opened, it opened wide enough for me and my three children, who I hadn't seen in a year, to walk right through. His family seemed to have known that his behavior was irrational. They noticed that I feared him and that he had begun accusing me of talking to his brothers and his father. When his parents would hear him fighting me, his father would enter the room and try to stop him. After one such incident, his brother started staying over to keep peace. His parents were elderly and family members were very concerned about their health. They petitioned the court to have their son evaluated. They succeeded in getting him into a veteran's hospital. It was while he was undergoing evaluation that I was able to leave in peace.

CHAPTER 5 – FREE! FREE! FREE! AT LAST

I WAS FINALLY FREE! It wasn't easy. I was first taken to the hospital to be examined. For the very first time in two years I was able to see a doctor for the scars and bruises that I had suffered. I was told that my ribs were fractured. Bones in my hand were cracked. My face had been broken in two places. I had a fractured skull. My back, breasts and stomach were completely covered with bite mark, and if that were not enough, my foot was infected from being bitten.

After the examination, I was informed that there was nothing that the doctors could do; the broken bones had healed themselves. I was given medicine and sent to a shelter for battered women.

On the way to the shelter, I inquired of the Lord if this was the right thing to do. I was reminded of the story of the man who was trapped on the roof of his house during a flood. He prayed for the Lord to deliver him. So the Lord sent a helicopter and a boat. But instead of taking them he said, "the Lord will provide. Go on." Well, the man died and went before the Lord. He accused God of not delivering him on time. It was then that the Lord reminded him of the helicopter and the boat. I left and I'm free.

Though I was free, I had to start over. I relocated to an area where I knew no one. Things were difficult at first. Especially the job market. Where I lived, the cost of living was cheaper, but there were fewer jobs available. I had to take a major cut in salary, but if you think about it, I really wasn't making anything before I got there because I was fired from my last job. I found a church to attend, which was a lot of help. My children were enrolled in school. While the expected stay in the shelter was normally one month, I was there for only three weeks. Going in, I was determined that I was going to move out of that shelter as soon as possible. I wanted to get on with my life, for me and my children. God must have felt the same way because he helped me along the way. Before I knew it, I was away from my ex-spouse for two months. I had my own place to live. I was employed again. This was also the place where I met the man I never thought that I deserved: my present husband. .

While my story of finding myself and escaping abuse ultimately sounds easy, it wasn't as easy as it appears. The main thing to remember is that it can be done. I have had flashbacks and thoughts of my first husband finding me. But I have held onto the thought, "I know that the Lord didn't bring me this far to leave me." That was my strength. I know where I was before I was abused. Now, I am determined to be even better.

I stayed away from the city where I was born and raised (also where I met my abuser) for more than three-and-a-half years before returning. I stayed away, not because I was afraid, but because God was preparing me for the work that I am in now. When I did return, I believed I still had transforming to do. However, I found that it had all been taken care of. God fixed it all.

New Beginnings

After the abuse, there were trials to endure and obstacles to overcome. Because of this, many women won't come out of abusive relationships. When the decision to leave is made, fear sets in. A woman gives much thought to such things as loneliness, survival, starting over, their children. Others have described to me similar mental anguish. Fear has been controlling battered women for so long that when they finally have nothing compelling them to return to abusive relationships, they go back anyway. This is why it is imperative that we learn to minister to these women and support them in their decisions. Some women may return to an abusive relationship up to 10 times before they finally break it off for good.

A woman's trials are often not over once she reaches refuge. She often becomes a victim of her new surroundings. This is due to her failure to confront the emotional and psychological difficulties resulting from the abuse. Instead of seeking proper counsel, the women continue as if they were never abused. Unknowingly, they can be controlled, intimidated, and violated by family members, friends, and yes, even pastors. This can result from them being forced to do things they are not comfortable with, making decisions they don't agree with, because they may capitulate to something as simple as an aggressive tone of voice. They are intimidated.

God forbid, but this can be especially true in the church. You will find many women who are content with where they are in their Christian life of "getting by." Not realizing that they are maintaining a false sense of peace. This spirit of control is in force when you have a controlling pastor heading the congregation. This controlling spirit is not evident of his being a strong leader. It comes from a residue of his past. Controlling spirits use fear, intimidation and aggressive language without concern for whether someone may get hurt. The main objective is to get done whatever they need to do, but their way. Some leaders are aware of the spirit of forcefulness but don't know what to do about it. Many times, in the scriptures, women are often interpreted as being under control of the man when, in fact, God created male and female in his image (Gen. 1:27).

While God expects us to obey **His** divine order, we are given an individual soul and are held responsible for "working out our own salvation with fear and trembling (Phil. 2:12)."

God's ways are not **grievous** (1John 5:3). Therefore, if you are in a relationship — church, job, or spouse — and you are unable to maintain a Christian stand and have the peace of God, you are not walking in obedience to God's word.

Chapter 6 – A Fresh Start

Here I was in a place that I had never been before, approximately 360 miles from where I was born and raised, surrounded by strangers.

The shelter was to be the beginning of my new start. I looked around, with an immediate sense of uncertainty. I wondered, "have I done the right thing by leaving?" Relocating to the shelter wasn't going to be easy. I thought about how I had left. I started to question whether I would be able to support my children, never mind myself.

I had left my husband several times before, but with no place to go and no means of survival, I returned. Time and again, I returned. But this time was different. This time, people knew what was going on. His family was involved. My family was involved. But why was I feeling sorry for him?!

I broke down and called him. He told me how much he missed me and he was so sorry that things got out of hand. But he blamed me that he was in the hospital. He told me how much I hurt him, that I turned his family away from him. He said how he really wanted to make it work, and how we were a family. He said I had no business in the shelter and he shouldn't be in the hospital.

"Please!" he pleaded. "Please, don't do this to us!"

I was crushed; feelings began to roll. Sorrow and hurt for this man rose in me. I decided to go back to him. This was what I told him but the Lord intervened. Within a split second my ex-husband reverted back to his former self. God showed me that this man hadn't changed, and that he was setting me up, perhaps even to kill me. He called me a liar. He threatened me, called me no good. He said I was using him, and there was no way I could be telling the truth about being faithful. He continued to call me out of my name and I said, "thank you, Lord."

I told him he hadn't changed, even over the telephone. I hung up, never to speak to him again. I couldn't believe that I was about to try to make it work one more time. I finally knew for sure that God had truly intervened to save me from my abusive marriage.

Now I knew that God wanted me free, but I was still uncertain as to what my next steps would be. I was in a shelter that was in his hometown but I was being considered for relocation. I had an option to go anywhere in the U.S. that I wanted. All I knew was that I wanted to go away. I needed a new start. It was a matter of finding a place.

Finally, the day arrived. I boarded a bus for a 45-minute ride to our new beginning. Three children, a couple of suitcases, $20, and a breath of fresh air. We made it. A taxi took us the final miles to a new start in a place where I knew no one, and no one knew me. A place I'd never been before.

One Day At A Time

We had arrived, my two daughters, my son and I. We were welcomed and given a tour of the facility. This shelter was different from the other one. It was situated in an old dormitory. In fact it was isolated and stood behind a mental institution. There were people of different ethnic backgrounds with children running and playing happily.

Our room had two beds and a crib. We shared an adjoining bathroom. It was welcoming and comfortable, but then something hit me. I hurried to the shelter director almost in a panic. I asked if I was allowed to go outside. She said sure. Away I went, just to walk around at first. I looked everywhere. I breathed the fresh air. I ran a little bit. I laughed. I said for the first time, "I am free." I thanked God, I thanked God and I thanked God.

This was a first step to my total recovery, and I was enjoying it!

Finally, it dawned on me that I no longer had to look over my shoulder. I was able to relax but not for long. That night as I lay in bed the devil was at his job. Mind games. Thoughts began to haunt me. All of the "what ifs," "How could I?" "Suppose he?" I would cry. Then I began to ask God for his strength. I knew this was going to be hard, but with the Lord I could make it.

Next, the counseling sessions were scheduled. I was welcomed by the counselor who would assist me. I was told how long I could expect to stay. They gave me a goal to set for getting settled. I was treated as a special case because I was from out of state and didn't have any family near. This automatically allowed me an extended stay beyond the required expected time. I was then told to look for a job.

I quickly realized I had to seek further counseling, away from the shelter. I needed life changing advice. The shelter counselor could indeed help me with my job hunting, the bus routes, and so on. But she could not give me the peace I needed at night. Peace could only come from God. I needed spiritual direction. What did I do? I immediately contacted the church.

Chapter 7 – Transition

I WAS IN THE SHELTER FOR THREE WEEKS. While I could have, and was expected to stay longer; this was not where I belonged. I needed a home for my children, now ages 6, 4, and 16 months. They needed a stable foundation and I couldn't give it to them at the shelter. I found a nice affordable two bedroom duplex. I rode by it every day while searching for a job. I found myself wondering how I would fit in this city. I knew that I didn't have a job yet, but somehow I knew that duplex was mine.

During my hunt for employment, I had to make sure my children ate, so I applied to social services for food stamps, Medicaid and financial assistance. This bothered me because I'd never requested these services before. I had been a member of the workforce. Then I understood why you should never say, "never." I needed the support at the time. It was the key to my family's survival.

In applying for the duplex, I encountered problem #1: my credit report. There was no way I could rent anything the way my credit report looked. But God saw me through. The duplex owner told me all he wanted was the first month's rent and deposit and I could move in. This was a blessing. I paid him from money I had received from social services. I had found a place for my children and me to live. This was our new home.

Shortly afterwards, I opened a line of communication with my parents. I decided against not letting anyone know where I was staying.

This was to be part of our new beginning. There were still feelings of pride, betrayal, confusion, and mistrust. I had been brainwashed by my husband to believe that my family was against me.

I called my mother, telling her my whereabouts. I told her I did not want to return to my hometown, which was Washington, D.C. I wanted a clean start and this is what the Lord gave me. Therefore, I would stay in North Carolina. My family understood, a blessing in itself. They now knew what I'd been through. They even helped me move to our new apartment and took my children home with them for the summer.

As a result of my parent's help, I was free to continue my search for a job. I was turned down many times. For example, I was selected for a position at a bank and then told that I couldn't qualify because of my credit. This hurt and could have been a major setback. While this was discouraging, I never stopped trusting the Lord. One of the biggest problems in trying to re-establish yourself is that you're not ready to trust people, even those who are trying to help. But I tried to fit in and within about two months I felt that I was going somewhere.

Strangers came to my home and furnished it. My children were being cared for by my parents. Things seemed to be coming together. But the job situation was hurting. I went to my room one day and wondered what it was all for. I called the church to thank them for the things they had done for me. After expressing my gratitude and appreciation I thought I detected a giggle in the voice of the church secretary. Whether I had or not, it upset me. I returned to my room and pulled out a bottle of pills. I felt I was no longer fit to live. Why was I still being abused, even after I had left the original place of abuse? Why was this man still haunting me? Why were others abusing me? I couldn't go on. I now knew my children would be cared for. There was nothing more for me. I wanted out.

But God intervened. He interrupted my agenda for his. I counted my blessings. It never failed that God visited me when things went wrong. I wouldn't let those few things turn me around. I picked myself up, dusted myself off and started over. With God's help I found a temporary position working for the county government.

This wasn't the end of my setbacks. As I started to get comfortable in my new surroundings, I experienced some things that I wasn't prepared for.

For instance, I would be watching television and would see a man hit a woman. I would feel for this woman. I would cry and sometimes I would have nightmares. I would think of him finding me. There was a time when I noticed a man sitting on the steps across from my home. From the distance he resembled my ex-husband. I watched him closely. After he sat there for a while, I called the police. By the time the police arrived, he had left. The police officer informed me that if indeed the man was my ex-husband he could not have arrested him. He told me that since we were still married, there was nothing the law could do. This really startled me. I asked if my husband needed to kill me before I could get the help I needed.

I was cautious from then on. I realized I didn't have the law on my side. I put extra locks on the doors to make sure we were safe. Whenever we attended church services, and there was a telecast we didn't stay. I was afraid that I would be seen on TV. It became frustrating, but I knew I had to suffer this out because this was better than what I had to go through while in that abusive relationship. At least I was free and the Lord was working on my mind.

I met my neighbors, and after a while I began to mingle. I realized that God had led me out and that he was not going to let my husband find me. The longer I stayed away the more comfortable I became with my new life. I was now able to learn how to live in my own home, comfortable with my children. Since the Lord had given me a job, there was much to do to fill an idle mind. Instead of sitting and daydreaming about what could happen I thought about making things happen for the good of my family. This helped me keep on striving and stop looking back.

CHAPTER 8 – CHURCH

I HAD MIXED EMOTIONS WHEN IT CAME TO THE CHURCH. The church had already sent me home to an abusive ex-husband. But I sought the Lord directly this time. Jesus was the only one who I knew could help me. I pledged to get my life together with Him. Meanwhile, people were very nice. The pastor took up several offerings for my family. I stayed awhile and the Lord blessed me. But I somehow was incomplete.

I knew that God had brought me out, and that he spared my life, but I couldn't go on as though this thing had never happened. I nevertheless felt the urge for a break. I needed to be out of the spiritual scene (not recommended) because I didn't know how to apply the spiritual to help the flesh. All I knew was that the church — the organization — was not helping me to understand the emotions I was feeling. No one was there to tell me that these emotions were natural and that most of all, I was human.

I still had a long way to go. I found myself lonely and despairing. I began to rationalize with God. I needed justification for my failure to stay in the church. I felt I deserved to backslide because I had suffered so much for so long. I decided to go back into the world.

I had long returned to smoking. My nerves were so shot from the abuse I felt I needed something. I also started occasionally drinking. I returned to a world of sin. But God never left me. I continued to pray even though I knew I was not living right. I knew my troubles and my pain were not because of God not loving me. Never once did I blame God for what I was feeling.

Sin became my way of handling my problems. If I fit in the world then it wouldn't be a problem if I drank, smoked, and cheated as my ex-husband accused me of. I was doing what was expected because I was in sin.

CHAPTER 9 – A NEW PARTNER

I MET A LADY at the shelter who had left her husband. She returned home only to find that he, too, would return and cause more trouble. I let her stay with me for a few days because my children were not at home. We both had been in the church and were living on the edge. We decided that we would go out on the town. I hadn't been to a nightclub in over five years.

We dressed and got on the bus. When we arrived, the club was closed but some people we met told us of another club. We decided to walk to the other club that was a few blocks away. We paid a cover charge and went in and sat at a table that centered around the dance floor.

We ordered drinks and talked for a few minutes. Then I saw this man across the room. I was instantly attracted to him. I could tell that he was tall and nice looking. I somehow felt that he was the man that I would spend my life with. I told my friend that I wasn't going to move until I met him. I sat there and willed him to come over. Finally, he came from across the dimly lit room and asked me to dance. I was so happy and danced so hard that my belt kept coming off! On the dance floor I could tell that he was a little older than me but he already had my heart. A change in the tempo caused us to dance closer. When he put his arms around me, I felt that I belonged right there. Thinking back, I would say I loved him before I knew him.

This is where I met my soul mate. We got to know each other well after that. I explained to him what was going on in my life. My children returned home after being with my parents and I introduced my new mate to them. We had been seeing each other for over a year, and I knew that I hadn't gotten a divorce and I was unclear as to whether I was to get one. I needed to know. Before I got into the relationship, I tried to find out if I had scriptural grounds for a divorce. It seemed that every Christian I went to didn't know either, or said I could based on him being abusive. I couldn't forget the Scripture that says, "for the woman which hath an husband is bound by the law to her husband so long as he liveth; (Romans 7:2).

I began to seek God's face; I felt the spirit of the Lord calling me back unto righteousness. I knew that I had met a man who made me very happy for the first time in my life and here I was unsure of what to do. I knew that according to the law I needed to be away from my ex-husband for one year to obtain a divorce. I managed that. Now I needed a word from the Lord, and He gave it to me.

God allowed me to see that I had chosen the man that I married, and he would not leave me alone if I continued to stay married to him. He thought of me as being property. Ephesians 5:28-29 says, "so ought men to love their wives as their own bodies. He that loveth his wife loveth himself. For no man ever yet hated his own flesh; but nourisheth and cherisheth it, even as the Lord the church."

This scripture assured me that my ex-husband's abusive behavior was not acceptable to God. You don't hurt the people you love. If you were connected as one then for sure you wouldn't hurt yourself. Now that I was free as to whether I should get a divorce, I was stuck on whether I should remarry.

In the meantime, God had strengthened this relationship that I was now in. He had begun ministering to me about coming back into the fold. I knew that I wasn't living right, but God told me to "come unto him all ye that labor and are heavy laden" (St. John 11:28). He said he would give me rest. God led us both back to church. This new man in my life had also been brought up in the church and had strayed. I joined his family church.

Although this is not a recommended way to meet the person God has for you, in this situation, God is glorified!

More Healing To Be Done

This may seem like effecting major change in a short time. I had gotten out of an abusive relationship and within two months I had met and fallen in love with someone new. One year later, pregnant and carrying my fourth child, we got married.

My new husband, who also had a 15 year-old son, was different in many ways but I found myself being very defensive. I had made up my mind that I was not going to be abused anymore by anyone. I needed control of my life. This caused some problems. I remember working on a temporary job and the supervisor said certain things that offended me. For perhaps the first time, I spoke up and protested. This happened at least twice with two different supervisors. My time was short from there. It wasn't long before my assignment was up. I was not re-hired but it didn't matter because I stood my ground.

I became very short tempered with people. I erected a shield so that no one could get in to hurt me. Many of us will do this without realizing it. I had no idea of the emotional state I was in. I only knew that I would not be hurt again. I became overly protective of my children. It led to an incident in which my new husband and I argued and I pushed him. He pushed me back. I called my mother and told her that I was leaving him. No man was going to hit me again. She told me that I shouldn't have pushed him. In my mind, I just wanted to get the first strike. I took time to think about what I had done and I apologized.

No one told me that I would be filled with so many mixed emotions. I had bottled up my feelings and proceeded with my life as though there had never been a change. I really needed help. I was much too proud to turn to a psychiatrist. I thought they were for other people, not me! I looked to the Lord to help me sort out my feelings. I began to pray for myself. Seeking the face of God as to why my heart was so heavy.

I visited my mother, joining my children already there. At that time I was about 6-months pregnant. When I got there I called and saw friends I hadn't seen in a while. After about three days I became very anxious. I felt paranoid. I didn't understand what was going on with me. I knew that I was supposed to stay longer, but I couldn't. I felt as if things were closing in on me. I became claustrophobic. I needed to go home. I realized I was in the city where I had been abused, and I was with family members who I hadn't forgiven because I buried my feelings. Finally I realized there was a problem within myself that I needed to clear up but I didn't know how. I continued to dislike confrontations so running away was much easier.

I failed to realize that I had become dependent upon my new environment and husband. I had covered up what I was feeling emotionally about my family and friends who lived in the area where the abuse took place. I didn't fully understand at the time what was happening to me. If I didn't live in the area anymore I didn't have to deal with what was in my head. I could erase the pain and suffering by again escaping the area of my abuse.

My new husband wired me some money to take the bus back to North Carolina but my parents took me home. While I was glad to be at my parent's home, I still hadn't dealt with my emotions.

CHAPTER 10 – ROAD TO RECOVERY

I WAS NOW LEARNING how to handle constructive criticism from friends without feeling as if they were trying to control me. Nevertheless, this was a major problem in my new marriage. I trusted my new husband. I trusted his judgment but I couldn't handle his criticism. Whenever he suggested that I could or could not do a certain task, I was offended. I thought he was trying to take control of my life. At one point I decided that I would physically make my point. I would push him or try to provoke him to fight me because I was determined that I would not be put in bondage ever again. Therefore, I would attack him. This of course only made matters worse.

I continued to pray and ask God to please help me. I knew that I was unstable in my actions. I started to feel insecure.

My new husband's actions didn't help much either. I had shared my experiences with him and I began to feel that he was taking advantage of me, given what he knew. Paradoxically, this loving wonderful man became emotionally abusive. He began to show a sense of control that I was all too familiar with. This time would be different though. Although still unstable in some ways, I had truly learned from my previous relationship. I began to really seek God. Unbeknownst to me, this was the test that would top all. How would I survive with a man I love and I know beyond any shadow of doubt God gave me? The only way I knew how was to trust God and follow His direction. This wouldn't be easy.

My new husband and I would argue over money, my whereabouts, children, bills, and our different lifestyles, or things that many couples argue about. There would be outbursts, where I would yell at him, he at me. I would cry, try to fight him, and God would make me go back and apologize to him. I spent many nights praying. I took time out of my lunch schedule at work to pray.

My husband decided one day that he would stop going to the church we were now attending. That was fine until he stopped going to church completely. It was not long before trouble was again stirred up.

Harsh words were spoken. He made demands, among them that I would pay most of our bills and he would make sure we had a place to live. I felt that I was being used, but God wouldn't let go. I tried to make ends meet. Checks began to bounce. I began working overtime. The outbursts at home became worse. We would still argue. If the food was short, he blamed me. When a bill didn't get paid, he blamed me. I had taken all I could. I was ready to give up. God intervened.

During this time God had birthed a prayer ministry in my spirit. I had an all night prayer line. People would call on the telephone at all hours. I had a true heart for helping people. I didn't want anyone to suffer. One of the major mistakes that I made was that I didn't know how to separate the ministry from my home where it wouldn't disturb my family life. Blindly, I was doing good deeds but my family was suffering. This caused problems with my husband.

I was at the end of my rope. I thought I must have missed God again. I couldn't go further like this. I continued praying and heard the Lord say to me that he would teach me how to live in the house with my husband in peace. He would show me how to win my husband.

With instruction from the Word, I prayed without ceasing (I Thess. 5:17). The Lord allowed my husband and I to come together and talk about our differences and to see where God would really make the difference in our marriage if we let him. God did. My husband returned to church and the healing began.

I learned how to live with another in peace and harmony. I learned to give up my will to the Lord's will. If I was right and my husband was wrong, and it didn't matter either way, I accepted the wrong for the sake of peace. I learned how to let God control my emotions and my feelings. I gave them over to the Lord. This was not easy. There would still be outbursts, but I learned that I did not have to become violent to deal with the situation. I could stand up for what I thought was right, but I learned to communicate righteously. I found that no one likes to argue alone. Silence could be your best friend in steamy situations while learning to apply the word "a soft answer turns away wrath." (Proverbs 15:1)

I learned how to apply God's word using wisdom. I now understand that there would be differences in a marriage. You may not always like your mate. This is a part of getting to know the person. I learned that aggressive attributes produce character boldness for God if temperance is applied. Our biggest problem was learning how to stop blaming one another for circumstances. The Bible says, "a house divided against itself cannot stand" (St. Matthew 12:25). We needed to come together.

I asked God "why was I the one who seemed to make all of the sacrifices?" "Why did I have to take the blame for things I didn't do?" God showed me that if we begin to examine ourselves first instead of making a judgment against our mates then we would be a little more tolerant of the other person's deficiencies. After all, we are not perfect, and we all have a long way to go.

From this point on things seemed to improve. We were now discussing situations in our relationship instead of being demanding towards one another. We were able to share our feelings about things that were said that could have damaged our marriage. More than ever we became flexible. Realizing that differing opinions didn't make either of us wrong allowed me to understand that my husband had his way of doing things, which didn't mean he was using force or control. God showed me that just like he had to work on me, he had to work on my husband.

Moving On

The Lord began to bless us from every direction. Our house was back in order. The job that I really wanted finally came through, but it wasn't what I had anticipated. I had waited for this job and now I didn't enjoy it, although it was a permanent job. I discussed with my husband the possibility of me coming home from this job and looking for another. He was all for it. Since the salary was not great, we decided that I would begin looking for work from home.

I quit after returning from vacation visiting my family. We really enjoyed ourselves. During the vacation, the Lord put our hearts and minds together. I began thinking about living back in my home area. I thought about what I could do to help those who were in the shelters, how I could take some classes and learn how to counsel others. I never thought of the abuse. I saw only the potential of helping someone else. I never thought about myself. My fears and uneasiness were in the past. Both my husband and I began to have similar thoughts of how we could help people who need help in Washington, D.C.

During the ride home to North Carolina, my husband and I began to talk about how we enjoyed ourselves, and how it felt to be going back to work. Much to my surprise — we began to think along the same line — my husband asked me how I would feel if we came to D.C. I asked him if this was what he wanted to do. He said that it might be worth a try. He thought that we could probably be successful in the move. He continued to talk and during the six-hour journey, we decided to move. We decided to start looking for a job for me. Meanwhile, my husband quit his job and also began to look for another. This was our time. We would both start anew. The way things went after that proved to be the hand of God. We made preparations to move in with my parents until we found a place of our own. The move was smooth. Everything fell in place. This was going to be the change we needed. We joined my sister and her children who were already living there. My brother was in and out because he was in college. The house was crowded but it was okay. My husband rode the bus back to our old home to get our furniture two days after we arrived.

While he was away, it finally happened, I came face to face with the emotions that I had buried. It was now time to deal with how I actually felt about my family's role during the abuse. I thought that they were guilty of not being there for me. I began to feel uneasy. I didn't say anything to anyone. I would get in the car and go for long rides. I visited different churches. I looked for scriptures that would imply we would be moving again soon. I stayed out as long as I could, returning home only to go to bed. When I would lie down, rest was impossible. I was unable to sleep. I tossed and turned all night long and I heard the voice of the Lord say, "you must forgive your family for whatever you think they did wrong to you."

I still had feelings of betrayal. I couldn't see my parents not knowing that I was in fear when I was being abused. I felt that they didn't do enough to help me while I was going through the abusive situation. I didn't understand that they only did what they knew to try and help. I needed to be delivered from my fears. I had accused my family of being responsible for taking me to court to have my children taken away. I was now confronted with these thoughts and no place to go.

Finally, I again yielded to the Holy Spirit. I told the Lord that I would try to get through this with help from Him. I learned to apply the same rule to my family as I did with my husband. I learned to accept people for the way they were. People usually react to the lifestyle they live. I began to see my own insecurities and faults and not judge people for what I thought were their weaknesses. As I began to look at my family members I saw that they did only what they knew to do. I accepted the fact that many people who have relatives in abusive relationships really don't know how to help them. Even though, we had different lifestyles, the Lord showed me their hearts. I was able to accept even those things that I wasn't sure they had done. This helped me not only to see my family differently but also those whom I thought were my friends.

During this difficult time, a significant thing happened. I was able to discuss the abuse with my parents. This was the beginning of the ending of my pain. This is where I finally discovered the erroneous information we shared. Our inability to reach out to each other was because of lack of understanding of one another. We all expressed the desire of wanting to comfort one another but we didn't know how. When the light finally went on, the walls of communication between my parents and I came down like the Berlin wall. It strengthened the relationship with my siblings. I never knew how or if I was going to overcome, but God knew that I would.

My husband was job hunting. I worked in a local fast food restaurant for about two months, but became sick. I was diagnosed with an incurable though not fatal disease. During my hospitalization, a new relationship with God began. During my illness I prayed each morning. I read and studied the Bible. I grew closer to God. This helped me to continue to confront my past. After six months, the Lord blessed us with an apartment

CHAPTER 11 – TIME FOR MINISTRY

IT WASN'T LONG BEFORE GOD would allow me to function in my calling. I had to get to a place spiritually where I could be utilized by Him. I was asked to take part in a documentary titled "Any Day Now" being produced out of Charlotte, N.C. It focused on 11 women who emerged from abusive relationships and who were now surviving. It emphasized them moving on to better lives, and making wiser decisions than before. In 1992, the film won the Documentary of the Year award from the National Radio and Television Awards. The ceremony was held in New York at the Waldorf Astoria Hotel. During the ceremony, the Lord showed me that I was part of that elegant surrounding. The banquet hall was breathtaking. I was dressed in beautiful clothing and knew I belonged in this kind of atmosphere. I told myself, "I am royalty!"

In route home, the Lord gave me the vision of conducting seminars. He put together the format and instructed me to get started. This was the beginning of "I Survived" Outreach Ministry. It was not easy. Pastors, Ministers, and church people were unwilling to admit abusive relationships could exist in their congregations. They were, like many others, unwilling to confront the issue. Most abused women never say anything. Some I spoke to said, "well, I'm praying that God will change him."

Like me, years before, they could not remove themselves from their situations, as horrible as they were. I wrote letters to 300 churches in the local area. I did not receive one response. I asked God how he expected me to help anyone when no one would respond. The Lord told me that he would open doors for me. I arranged a seminar and invited whoever would come. I sacrificed my finances and bought some radio airtime.

This worked. The Lord blessed and we had a full house. This stirred up strength and determination within me. I knew of many women who were being abused. Some were married to unsaved men; others were married to men within the church. After this session, things moved slowly while I built up a trusting relationship with these abused but suspicious women. Unfortunately, some had been helped before but never received follow-up services from the ministry. Abuse in the church was an old problem but a new topic. Many pastors will not deal with domestic violence in their congregations because of their own feelings of guilt, or they refuse to be responsible for family division. God again said, "in the fullness of time" I will bless. I continued helping where I was needed. I counseled individually and as the Lord led, I spoke at different churches.

The Lord continued to heal me as I moved along. I began to take classes to help me minister to church women who were being abused. I completed a course on Christian counseling. Using the Bible as my guide, I searched the scriptures for understanding of God's word to help direct and interpret scriptures that had been taken out of context concerning woman. I also attended seminars and conferences.

Preparing for the next step in this ministry, God instructed me to plan a conference for the people of God to come and learn how to approach domestic violence in the church. October is National Domestic Violence Awareness Month, but there was nothing to help women in the church. God told me to coordinate a meeting place for the body of Christ, and he would do the rest. I conducted my first conference in October 1995. I have held them ever since. Awareness in the church is beginning to develop as the days go by. However, there is still more work to be done.

Jesus Christ has set me free. He led me through the Dead Sea to a land of milk and honey. I am now happily married to the man that God has given me. He is the perfect God-fearing husband and father I had sought. Since returning to my hometown, I can go back into the same areas where I was once abused. I no longer have fear and can hold my head up high because I am no longer in bondage. I know that my abuser can also come to this city any time he feels like it but that does not bother me because I know that part of my life is over forever.

During my time of trial I lost my job with the U.S. government. After returning home God has seen fit to guide me to be reinstated in the government, and even making much more money than when I left. My children are stable and are all honor roll students. They are growing in the Lord, and truly know what it means to have a father who loves them.

Today, I pastor Survival Temple Church. I assist church leaders with setting up domestic violence outreach ministries in the local church. I train clergy who will assist and counsel battered women. I also conduct a seminar entitled, "Breaking the Cycle of Domestic Violence within the Body of Christ." Since the Lord has brought me out of bondage, I have a yearning to address not only those who don't know Him as their personal savior. I want all to know that abuse in not acceptable to God under any conditions. This behavior cannot go on in the church. There are many people, including clergy, who are aware of abuse and don't know how to deal with it. God has given me patience, which is a beneficial asset in counseling, and first hand knowledge of what it means to be abused. I am here to let you know that help is available. Help is all around us. We must become educated to what God has given us and use it.

This book was written to enlighten and strengthen the women of God, both those who are standing in the shadows and those who have been delivered. God has not given us the spirit of fear but of power, and of love, and of a sound mind (2 Tim. 1:7).

"I Survived" is dedicated to the women who are persevering to be obedient to the Lord, and revere His divine order.

Deliverance, grace and mercy allows me to tell my story in order to help others who might be in a similar situation as mine, or, now that they have been delivered, are wondering what they can do to help others.

I have been out of the abusive relationship for more than 17 years and have continued to work in the domestic violence ministry. In January 2006, I devoted my life to full time ministry. I am now a contact person to various domestic violence shelters in the area for those who have concerns about counseling a woman of God. I have also been able to help ministers and pastors to encourage the abused women in their local churches

I finally have it: the closeness, the joy, the peace and yes, the security that I longed for in the Lord. The time has finally come when I feel complete and settled in Jesus. I knew even on the worst days that God loved me and that He would never let anything happen to me that I couldn't bear. I knew that He was with me every step of the way. I know that I could not have made it through everything that I suffered, everything that I endured, without God. No one could have convinced me that I would be able to survive the pain, suffering, verbal, physical, mental, and spiritual abuse that I have gone through. To God be the glory: I made it. **I SURVIVED! YOU CAN TOO.**

Epilogue

Survival Strategies

As you can see the road to success after abuse is not as easy as it may appear. However, it can be done. With God all things are possible.

When making plans to leave domestic violence, major strategies have to be considered. This will successfully reduce the chances of returning. A plan of escape and if possible a buddy system with someone you can trust are essential. It is very important to maintain personal papers such as birth certificates, social security cards and health records. Also, any background information on the perpetrator would be extremely helpful when seeking legal assistance. It is not recommended to seek shelter with relatives or friends that the perpetrator knows. Victims who are serious about leaving and never returning should consider moving as far away as possible. This lessens the ability for her abuser to find them and allows them to experience a true sense of freedom when considering options of returning.

Making the decision to leave can be hard based on the mixed emotions the victim is experiencing. No doubt, the perpetrator is telling her how much he loves her, he needs her, and how he won't do it again. Fear is ever present. The decision to divorce is being considered especially if there are any children involved. She could also still love him and not want her family divided. These feelings and emotions are valid. The woman in the church thinks of her husband's status. She doesn't want to make him look bad. She is taught that what goes on at home should stay in the home. The bible says, "whatever is done in darkness will come to the light" (1Cor. 4:5). Who better to bring it out than the victim. This will not only help her, but it may cause him to get the help he needs to keep the family together.

Although many victims are women there are men who are being abused. The abuse weighs the same. No one should live in a home with a person and not be free. Men must help other men. If women help women and they become freed, what about the men? The house is yet divided until he gets the help he needs.

Abuse is running rampant in our local churches, and we need to acknowledge and deal with it. The bible says, "we are to submit to one another," we are joint heirs together with Christ. When you (men) take on a wife, the two become one flesh, you must treat your wife as Christ loves the church, and He gave his life for us (Ephesians 5:21,25,31&33).

In order for the woman of God to gain enough strength and courage to come out of domestic violence she must first seek the face of God. One thing that is pertinent to her survival is prayer. She must realize that God is not the perpetrator. God did not give her this individual. God is not the author of confusion.

Secondly, she must confess her faults no matter how small. If she knows that marrying this person was out of the will of God, she needs to repent. This prepares her for total sanctification before God. Lastly, she must surrender to God. This will say to God, not my will, but your will be done in my life.

She must not focus on her perpetrator; she must practice the presence of God. In essence she must dwell on how God would want her to live. Would God want her to suffer this way? She needs to study the word of God and begin to see herself as God sees her. Find scriptures of strength to hold on to. Know that God says, you are "fearfully and wonderfully made" (Psalm 139:14); "you are a royal priesthood, a peculiar people" (1Peter 2:9). The Bible also declares that "God will never leave you nor forsake you" (Heb. 13:5).

This will help her to learn who she is in the sight of God. The perpetrator has put her down and damaged her self-esteem. Now, she must allow the Word of God show her that she is special, that she is fearfully and wonderfully made (Psalm 139:14).

Following this method will surely encourage her spiritually, and will allow her to see herself in a different light. No matter how many bruises she has, she should wash her face and see what God sees, beauty. Beauty is not only outward. The woman was not an after thought. God made her compatible to man with emphasis that he give to her, which assisted in taking his mind off of himself. She also has power, only to be tapped into.

Are You Being Abused?

Every twelve seconds in this country a woman is beaten or injured by the man she lives with and loves. More women seek emergency treatment for injuries caused by their husbands or partners than from rape, car accidents and muggings combined. This abuse is particularly heinous when it exists with the Body of Christ. I can tell you from my own experience that sincere and committed women of God are being abused in the name of the Lord. Misinterpretation of scriptures such as, "likewise ye wives be in subjection…" (1Peter 3:1) has heightened the defense of the perpetrator. Scriptural misinterpretation and gender orientation can mislead and cause harm if we fail to rightly divide the word of God.

While it is true that God has a divine order, we are to revere one another. We must use wisdom and knowledge if we are to be accordance with the Word of God. The Bible says, in Ephesians 5:25, "husband, love your wives, even as Christ also loved the church and gave himself for it."

Abusers cause fear and confusion. God is not the author of confusion, but he has given us peace (1Corin. 14:33).
"For God hath not given us the spirit of fear; but of power and of love, and of a sound mind…" (2 Tim. 1:7). Abuse is contrary to the word of God. We are to acknowledge the Lord in all our ways and he will direct our paths.

If you are being abused, don't keep it a secret. Talk about it! The following questions are some ways to determine if you are a victim of abuse.

1. Does your mate keep track of all of your time?
2. Does your mate keep you isolated from outside contact?
3. Does your mate accuse you of being unfaithful?
4. Does your mate discourage your relationships with family and friends?
5. Does your mate prevent you from working or going back to school?
6. Does your mate criticize you or humiliate you in front of

others?
7. Does your mate anger easily without being provoked?
8. Does your mate belittle things that are important to you?
9. Does your mate hit, slap or punch you or your children?
10. Does your mate threaten to use a weapon against you?
11. Does your mate do bodily harm to you?
12. Does your mate force you to have sex against your will?

If you find yourself saying yes to any of these questions, you should seek help today. For shelter referrals, please call the Battered Women's Shelter in your area. This number can be found by dialing 411. If you are in immediate danger, please call 911.

Scriptural References

Genesis 3:16 ● St. Matthews 21:1-15 ● St. John 4:29
St. Matthews 21:2-3 ● I Peter 3:1 ● I Peter 2:9 ● I Timothy 2:11-12
St. Mark 8:34 ● Galatians 3:26-29 ● Genesis 2:24 ● Isaiah 54:17
Genesis 1:27 ● Philippians 2:12 ● I John 5:3 ● Romans 7:2
Ephesians 5:28-29 ● Ephesians 5:21, 25, 31 & 33 ● St. John 11:28
I Thessalonians 5:17 ● Proverbs 15:1 ● St. Matthews 12:25
Psalm 139:14 ● Hebrews 13:5 ● 2 Timothy 1:7 ● I Corinthians 4:5

Adrianne D. Brady

Adrianne D. Brady was born and raised in Washington, DC. She is married and the mother of five. She is the founder of I Survived Outreach Ministry and pastor of Survival Temple Church located in Capitol Heights, M.D.

Pastor Brady was married to a preacher who abused her for two years. While in the abusive relationship and seeking help from various churches she realized the help for the woman in the church was and still is very limited. She found herself seeking a Godly answer and wasn't very successful. Different pastors told her that she should go home and work on her marriage. After the Lord delivered her, she was led of God to go back to help the women who are being left out (the women in the church).

Through this experience she started conducting seminars, workshops, and an annual conference entitled "Breaking the Cycle of Domestic Violence in the Body of Christ." This also initiated the writing of her book "I Survived: True Encounter of a Battered Woman" and the start of I Survived Outreach Ministry.

Pastor Brady has traveled extensively over the years speaking on the issue of domestic violence in the church. She has participated in various women's meetings and programs. Her speaking engagements have taken her throughout the Baltimore-Washington area as well as Virginia, Pennsylvania, Delaware, Massachusetts, Missouri, Ohio, etc. She has participated in panel discussions representing clergy and domestic violence as well as board meetings of local shelters. She was also contacted by the Oprah Winfrey Show and appeared in a Documentary called "Any Day Now" in Charlotte, N.C.

Through the leading of the Holy Ghost, Pastor Brady has comprised a training package specifically for the Body of Christ which also includes her latest book, How to Counsel the Abused Woman in the Church. Churches who are interested in starting a domestic violence outreach center in their local church would find Pastor Brady's training and expertise in this area very helpful. If you would like to speak to Pastor Brady, please feel free to contact her at (202) 644-6741 or email: adriannebrady@yahoo.com.

www.ingramcontent.com/pod-product-compliance
Lightning Source LLC
Chambersburg PA
CBHW031213090426
42736CB00009B/906